COOKING

THE

NORWEGIAN

WAY

Lerner Publications Company
A division of Lerner Publishing Group
241 First Avenue North
Minneapolis, MN 55401 U.S.A.

Website address: www.lernerbooks.com

Library of Congress Cataloging-in-Publication Data

Munsen, Sylvia.
      Cooking the Norwegian way / by Sylvia Munsen.—Rev. & expanded.
         p.   cm. — (Easy menu ethnic cookbooks)
      Includes index.
      Summary: Introduces the land, culture, and cuisine of Norway and
   includes recipes for such foods as rice pudding, open-face sandwiches,
   and whipped cream cake.
      ISBN: 0–8225–4118–1 (lib. bdg. : alk. paper)
      1. Cookery, Norwegian—Juvenile literature. 2. Norway—Social life
   and customs—Juvenile literature. [1. Cookery, Norwegian. 2. Norway—
   Social life and customs.] I. Title. II. Series.
   TX722.N6 M86 2002
   641.59481—dc21   2001003276

Manufactured in the United States of America
1 2 3 4 5 6 – AM – 07 06 05 04 03 02

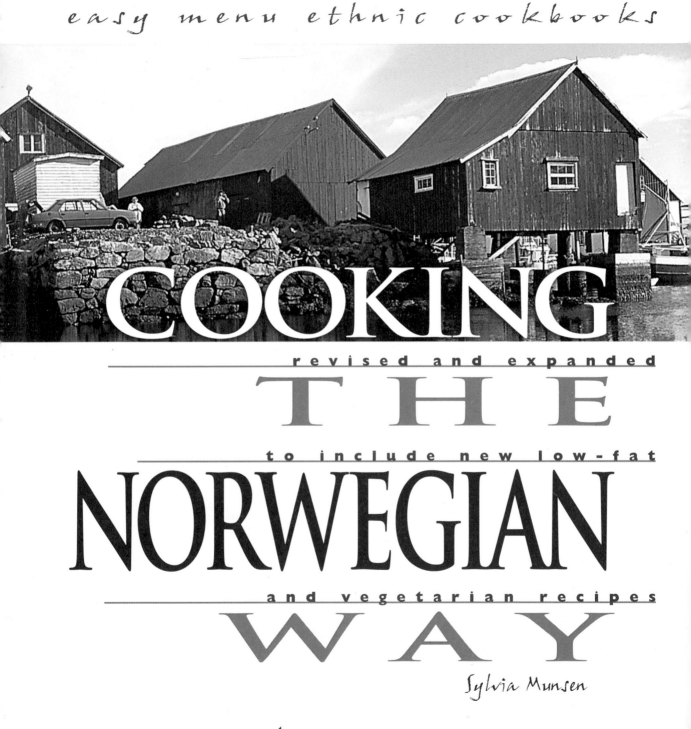

easy menu ethnic cookbooks

COOKING

revised and expanded

THE

to include new low-fat

NORWEGIAN

and vegetarian recipes

WAY

Sylvia Munsen

Lerner Publications Company • Minneapolis

Contents

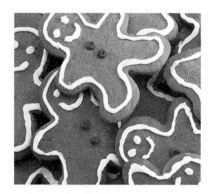

Introduction

Norwegian cooking has been shaped by the country's landscape, climate, and natural resources. Coastal waters provide ample fish, a staple of the Norwegian diet. The many hours of light during summer allow for a slow ripening of berries and fruits, giving them a special flavor. Sheep graze in the mountains, providing meat that can be eaten fresh or dried, cured, and preserved for the very long winter. Cows produce milk, "the mother of all dishes" in Norway.

Some Norwegian dishes, such as boiled potatoes and baked fish, are familiar. Other foods are not as well known outside Norway, but they are tasty to eat and easy to make. Once you know about some of the foods and customs, you'll want to try making your own Norwegian meals. Then you can go on to the best part—eating!

Norwegians enjoy using fresh fruits for tasty treats such as whipped cream cake. (Recipe on page 56.)

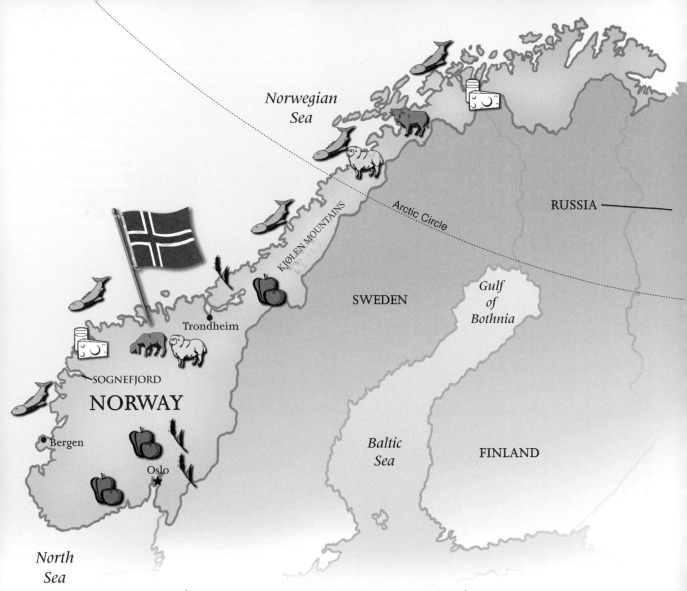

Norwegian
Sea

Arctic Circle

RUSSIA ——————

KJØLEN MOUNTAINS

SWEDEN

Gulf
of
Bothnia

Trondheim

SOGNEFJORD

NORWAY

Baltic
Sea

FINLAND

Bergen

Oslo

North
Sea

The Land and Its People

Norway remains a land of unspoiled natural beauty. Perched atop the globe, the long, narrow country stretches about 1,100 miles from north to south but is often no more than 60 miles wide from east to west. Steep, jagged fjords, salmon-filled rivers, plummeting waterfalls, snow-crested mountains, miles of coast, and green meadows and farmland create a varied and dramatic landscape.

Water has always affected Norway's history and culture. This is because about two-thirds of Norway is surrounded by the sea, and hundreds of fjords jut inland along the coast. A fjord is an arm of the sea that reaches into the mountains. Some fjords are many miles long—the longest, Sognefjord, stretches about 125 miles. Since most of Norway is rocky and mountainous, Norwegians depend on the fjords and the sea for both transportation and food.

Farming is also important in Norway, even though only about 5 percent of the land can be used to grow crops. Family farms in Norway are small. But the livestock, grains, vegetables, and fruits raised in Norway form the major staples of the Norwegian diet.

The northern part of Norway, called the "land of the midnight sun," lies above the Arctic Circle. In the summer, the sun shines twenty-four hours a day, followed by twenty-four hours of darkness in winter. Even in southern Norway, summer days are long and winter nights last more than seventeen hours.

Norway is a modern, technologically advanced country, but Norwegians are also deeply attached to nature. People of all ages spend as much time as possible outdoors, skiing, hiking, fishing, and biking, and city dwellers escape to their cabins in the wilderness whenever possible.

The Food

Norwegian farmers grow rye, wheat, and barley on their small amount of available land. These grains are used to make many kinds of bread. Farmers also raise sheep, goats, pigs, and dairy cattle, which provide mutton, lamb, and pork, as well as the cheeses that Norwegians enjoy. Two special Norwegian cheeses are *geitost*, which is made from goat's milk, and *gammelost*, a tangy brown cheese made from soured skim milk.

Fruits and vegetables are other products grown in Norway. This may seem odd, since one-third of the country lies above the Arctic

Circle. But the warm Gulf Stream currents and mild southwesterly winds keep the average temperature in Norway higher than that of other northern lands.

Norway is cool and damp during the growing season. Vegetables that grow well in this climate are potatoes, carrots, cauliflower, cabbage, peas, and rutabagas. A Norwegian dinner often includes potatoes, especially boiled potatoes. Novelist Knut Hamsun paid tribute to the prominent place of the potato in Norway, writing, "A man may be without bread, but if he has the potato he will not starve." At least twelve different kinds of potatoes grow in Norway.

Many kinds of berries thrive in Norway, including strawberries, blueberries, lingonberries (also known as mountain cranberries), and cloudberries. Cloudberries are bright orange and shaped like raspberries. They are called cloudberries because they grow in the mountains, "near the clouds." They are sometimes mixed with cream in a dish called *multekrem*.

Because they live so close to the sea, Norwegians eat a lot of fish. The waters surrounding Norway are rich with *torsk* (cod), herring, pollack, haddock, mackerel, and other types of fish. Salmon is abundant in the rivers along the coast and is also raised on fish farms. Norway is one of the world's leading producers of salmon, which is exported to Europe and the United States.

In the summer, Norwegians can buy fresh fish daily at the outdoor fish markets. The most plentiful fish in the markets is torsk, which is practically the national fish of Norway. It is called "poor man's lobster."

In the days before refrigerators and freezers existed, Norwegians needed to find ways to store fish and meat for the long winter. They preserved fish and meat in a number of ways—drying, salting, curing, pickling, and smoking. Although people no longer rely on cured and dried meats and fish for survival, they are still a popular part of Norwegian cuisine. Dried cod that is soaked in water and lye is called *lutefisk*. Some Norwegians consider lutefisk a delicacy, while others hate it!

A fish market in the coastal town of Bergen provides fresh fish for Norwegian cooking.

Although fish is important in Norway, Norwegian cooking is known for its use of many different types of food. The Vikings (A.D. 700 to A.D. 1000), the early seafaring Norwegian explorers, are said to have started the smorgasbord, a buffet of a wide variety of dishes.

The smorgasbord, a Norwegian favorite, offers meats, cheeses, bread, soups, and other foods.

According to legend, the Vikings always brought back a variety of foods from their voyages. But they never brought enough for everybody to have a full helping, so people at home only got a small taste of each food. A typical smorgasbord includes many kinds of fish, cold sliced meats, cheeses, vegetables, salads, breads, and a hot dish such as meatballs or meatcakes. Dessert may be fresh fruit, cold fruit soup, or rice pudding. Buffets such as these are often served in hotels and restaurants.

One of the oldest Norwegian food dishes is porridge. Until the mid-1800s, Norwegians ate porridge twice or even three times a day. An old tale from Telemark, a southern province of Norway, says that each woman in the area was asked if she could make porridge. If the answer was "No," she was told, "You may as well pack up." In other words, if you couldn't make porridge, you were of no use!

Ordinary porridge, such as rice porridge, may be eaten for breakfast. A richer porridge called *rømmegrøt*, made with flour and sour cream, is eaten for holiday meals and family celebrations.

Holidays and Festivals

Like the foods in Norway, holidays and festivals reflect the cycles of nature. "We use our holidays to celebrate the sun," wrote Norwegian author and explorer Thor Heyerdahl. "We celebrate the arrival of the sun, the summer solstice, we journey to the mountains in search of the sun, and on the day we miss it most, because it is farthest away, we cheer ourselves with a grand Christmas feast."

In ancient times, a midwinter feast, called Jul in Norwegian, was a festival of lights to mark the transition from the dark winter to spring and summer. It was a time to celebrate the harvest and the cycles of birth and death. Starting about A.D. 1000, the yearly feast was turned into a Christian holiday, Christmas, marking the birth of Jesus. Some of the ancient traditions, such as the feasting and the lights, live on in the modern holiday.

Preparations begin for Christmas throughout Norway in December. A special Christmas beer, *juleøl*, is brewed, people do their Christmas shopping, and families and friends get together to celebrate at work, home, and school. In many homes, an enticing spicy aroma fills the air as families bake the traditional seven types of Christmas cookies, along with *julekake*, sweet Christmas bread.

Christmas trees are decorated with white lights or candles, tinsel, small Norwegian flags, wood or straw ornaments, and colorful heart-shaped paper baskets. Children make these paper baskets, which are often filled with nuts, fruits, and other goodies. Many kids also hang up stockings.

The main festivities happen on Christmas Eve, December 24. Christmas dinner foods differ from one part of the country to another. In the coastal areas and in northern Norway, people eat cod, halibut, or lutefisk. In the eastern part of the country, pork ribs, sausages, and patties are on the menu, while people in western Norway prefer *pinnekjøtt*, salted lamb ribs. More and more Norwegians are turning to turkey, which is not as common in Norway as in other countries.

Many families have a bowl of porridge or rice pudding on Christmas Eve. An almond is hidden in the pudding, and whoever finds it gets a reward, usually a pig made of marzipan (sweet almond paste) or a piece of chocolate. That person is also supposed to have good luck and happiness in the new year. In other families, the person who gets the almond is in charge of the ceremonies on Christmas Eve.

An old tradition is to leave out a bowl of porridge for the *nisse*, a gnome or elf who was said to protect the farm. The nisse would be helpful as long as he got his Christmas porridge—if not, he might cause trouble. There's also the *julenissen*, or Christmas gnome, sort of like a Norwegian Santa Claus. The julenissen has a long white beard and wears a red stocking cap, knee-length britches, and a Norwegian sweater. The julenissen hands out presents to the children on Christmas Eve.

After dinner, the family joins hands and walks around the Christmas tree, singing carols. The presents are opened, and as the kids play with their new toys, the adults enjoy coffee and Christmas cookies.

On Christmas Day, Norwegians typically prepare a smorgasbord, with foods such as ham, herring in tomato sauce, sausages, pork patties, salads, and desserts. In many parts of the country, lobster is served for breakfast.

Easter in Norway, besides being a religious holiday, is a celebration of solitude, a time to "commune with nature." Even though snow still covers the ground, the days are getting longer and the sun

A Christmas tree decorates the main room of a Norwegian house during the winter holidays.

is stronger. Many Norwegians are off work for the week between Palm Sunday and Easter, and they go to the mountains to ski and stay in a cabin.

The true celebration of spring takes place on May 17, called Syttende Mai, or Constitution Day—the most important holiday in Norway. The day marks the anniversary of the country's declaration of independence from Denmark in 1814, when Norwegian elected officials signed a new constitution.

May 17 is a day of flags, parades, speeches, and bands playing the national anthem. Norwegians everywhere carry flags and wear the embroidered national costume. In Oslo the highlight of the day is

The city of Trondheim, Norway, welcomes visitors to its summer festival celebrating the legend of King Olav Haraldsson.

the children's parade, when thousands of schoolchildren, waving flags and banners, march past the Royal Palace in salute to the king. After the parade, local communities celebrate with speeches, games and contests, bands, and local parades. At night, people join friends or neighbors for parties.

Food on Constitution Day might include hot dogs and ice cream as well as the traditional holiday food, rømmegrøt (sour cream porridge). Many people also enjoy a glass of eggnog on May 17. At this early point in spring, the only fruit in season is rhubarb, so some people make a dessert with rhubarb—or buy a cake from the bakery.

The peak of summer is celebrated on Midsummer Eve, June 23. This festival marks the summer solstice, when the days are longest and the nights are light. All over the country, people make bonfires, barbecue, and party with friends. People might decorate their homes with birch branches and freshly cut flowers. Once again, rømmegrøt is on the menu.

A final summer festival, Olsok, or Saint Olav's Day, takes place on July 29. Olsok commemorates King Olav Haraldsson, one of Norway's earliest kings. On Saint Olav's Day, the city of Trondheim holds a Saint Olav Festival, and in nearby Stiklestad, where Olav died, thousands of visitors attend the Legend of Saint Olav, an outdoor play in which 300 actors, a choir, and an orchestra reenact the battle that took place there almost one thousand years ago.

Before You Begin

Cooking any dish, plain or fancy, is easier and more fun if you are familiar with its ingredients. Norwegian cooking makes use of some ingredients that you may not know. Sometimes special cookware is also used, although the recipes in this book can easily be prepared with ordinary utensils and pans.

The most important thing you need to know before you start is how to be a careful cook. On the following page, you'll find a few rules that will make your cooking experience safe, fun, and easy. Next, take a look at the "dictionary" of cooking utensils, terms, and special ingredients. You may also want to read the suggestions for preparing healthy, low-fat meals.

Once you've picked out a recipe to try, read through it from beginning to end. Now you are ready to shop for ingredients and to organize the cookware you will need. When you have assembled everything, you're ready to begin cooking.

Cucumber salad combines paper-thin slices of cucumber with tangy vinegar and fresh herbs. (Recipe on page 51.)

The Careful Cook

Whenever you cook, there are certain safety rules you must always keep in mind. Even experienced cooks follow these rules when they are in the kitchen.

- Always wash your hands before handling food. Thoroughly wash all raw vegetables and fruits to remove dirt, chemicals, and insecticides. Wash uncooked poultry, fish, and meat under cold water.
- Use a cutting board when cutting up vegetables and fruits. Don't cut them up in your hand! And be sure to cut in a direction *away* from you and your fingers.
- Long hair or loose clothing can easily catch fire if brought near the burners of a stove. If you have long hair, tie it back before you start cooking.
- Turn all pot handles toward the back of the stove so that you will not catch your sleeves or jewelry on them. This is especially important when younger brothers and sisters are around. They could easily knock off a pot and get burned.
- Always use a pot holder to steady hot pots or to take pans out of the oven. Don't use a wet cloth on a hot pan because the steam it produces could burn you.
- Lift the lid of a steaming pot with the opening away from you so that you will not get burned.
- If you get burned, hold the burn under cold running water. Do not put grease or butter on it. Cold water helps to take the heat out, but grease or butter will only keep it in.
- If grease or cooking oil catches fire, throw baking soda or salt at the bottom of the flame to put it out. (Water will *not* put out a grease fire.) Call for help, and try to turn all the stove burners to "off."

Cooking Utensils

cheese slicer—A flat metal utensil somewhat like a spatula with a sharp edge through the middle, used for cutting very thin slices of cheese

food processor—An electric appliance with a blade that revolves inside a container to chop, mix, or blend food

slotted spoon—A large spoon with holes in it to allow liquid to drain

waffle iron—An electric appliance with two metal parts that shut onto each other, pressing the waffle batter into a certain shape and cooking it. Norwegian waffle irons create five heart-shaped waffles.

whisk—A wire utensil used for beating food by hand

Cooking Terms

blanch—To partially cook a food in boiling water for a short time; also called *parboil*

boil—To heat a liquid over high heat until bubbles form and rise rapidly to the surface

brown—To cook food quickly in fat over high heat so that the surface turns an even brown

cream—To blend two or more ingredients (such as butter and sugar) together until the mixture has a creamy consistency

fold—To blend an ingredient with other ingredients by using a gentle overturning circular motion instead of by stirring or beating

hard cook—To boil an egg in its shell until both the yolk and white are firm

knead—To work dough by pressing it with the palms, pushing it outward and then pressing it over on itself

poach—To cook in a simmering liquid

preheat—To allow an oven to warm up to a certain temperature before putting food in it

sauté—To fry quickly over high heat in oil or fat, stirring or turning the food to prevent burning

scald—To heat a liquid (such as milk) to a temperature just below its boiling point

shred—To tear or cut food into small pieces, either by hand or with a grater

simmer—To cook over low heat in liquid kept just below its boiling point. Bubbles may occasionally rise to the surface.

steep—To soak in a liquid

Special Ingredients

agar-agar—A thickening agent made from sea vegetables

bay leaf—The dried leaf of the bay (also called laurel) tree. It is used to season food.

buttermilk—A milk product made from soured milk

candied fruit—Fruit that is encrusted with sugar or syrup

cardamom seed—A spice from the ginger family, either whole or ground, that has a rich color and gives food a sweet, cool taste

CHEESES

gammelost—A tangy brown cheese made from soured skim milk

geitost—A brown cheese made from goat's milk

Norwegian—A mild cheese that is similar to Gouda

chive—A plant that is related to onions and is used as a seasoning

cornmeal—A meal made from ground corn

cornstarch—A fine white starch made from corn, commonly used to thicken sauces and gravies

dill—An herb whose seeds and leaves (called dill weed) are both used in cooking. The flavor of the leaves is similar to that of parsley, and the flavor of the seeds resembles caraway seed.

gelatin—A clear, powdered protein substance used as a thickening agent

ginger—A spicy seasoning made from the dried and ground stem of a tropical herb

nutmeg—A fragrant spice, either whole or ground, that is often used in desserts

paprika—A red seasoning made from ground, dried pods of the capsicum pepper plant

peppercorns—The dried whole berries of a tropical vine, which are ground to form black and white pepper. Green peppercorns are the unripened berry, black peppercorns are dried, and white peppercorns are ripened and processed.

potato flour—A flour made from potatoes that have been cooked, dried, and ground. This flour is mainly used in gravies, breads, and cakes.

rutabaga—A yellow-fleshed root vegetable

smoked salmon—Raw salmon that has been preserved by exposure to smoke

stone-ground whole wheat flour—A flour from wheat that is ground under a millstone. It is called whole wheat because the bran is not removed from the grain.

tapioca—The roasted and ground root of the tropical cassava plant, used as a thickener or eaten as a pudding

white pepper—A seasoning made from ground peppercorns. White pepper is used when black pepper would make the food look less appealing.

yeast—An ingredient used in baking that causes dough to rise and become light and fluffy. Yeast is available either in small, white cakes called compressed yeast or in granular form called active dry yeast.

Healthy and Low-Fat Cooking Tips

Many cooks are concerned about preparing healthy, low-fat meals. Fortunately, there are simple ways to reduce the fat content of most dishes. Here are a few general tips for adapting the recipes in this book. Throughout the book, you'll also find specific suggestions for individual recipes—and don't worry, they'll still taste delicious!

Many Norwegian recipes call for butter. Using oil lowers saturated fat, but you can also reduce the amount of oil you use. Sprinkling a little salt on fish or vegetables brings out their natural juices, so less oil is needed. It's also a good idea to use a nonstick frying pan if you decide to use less oil than the recipe calls for.

Another common substitution for butter is margarine. Before making this substitution, consider the recipe. If it is a dessert, it's often best to use butter. Margarine may noticeably change the taste or consistency of the food.

Other dairy products, such as cream, milk, and sour cream, are also common in Norwegian cooking. An easy way to trim fat from a recipe is to use skim or evaporated skim milk in place of cream, whole milk, or 2 percent milk. In recipes that require sour cream, you may be able to substitute low-fat or nonfat sour cream, but lower-fat sour cream may change the consistency or taste of the food. Another possible substitution for sour cream is nonfat plain yogurt.

When a recipe calls for meat, such as sliced ham or ground beef, buy extra-lean meat to reduce fat. Norwegian cooking uses a lot of fish, which is naturally low in fat.

There are many ways to prepare meals that are good for you and still taste great. As you become a more experienced cook, try experimenting with recipes and substitutions to find the methods that work best for you.

METRIC CONVERSIONS

Cooks in the United States measure both liquid and solid ingredients using standard containers based on the 8-ounce cup and the tablespoon. These measurements are based on volume, while the metric system of measurement is based on both weight (for solids) and volume (for liquids). To convert from U.S. fluid tablespoons, ounces, quarts, and so forth to metric liters is a straightforward conversion, using the chart below. However, since solids have different weights—one cup of rice does not weigh the same as one cup of grated cheese, for example—many cooks who use the metric system have kitchen scales to weigh different ingredients. The chart below will give you a good starting point for basic conversions to the metric system.

MASS (weight)

1 ounce (oz.)	=	28.0 grams (g)
8 ounces	=	227.0 grams
1 pound (lb.) or 16 ounces	=	0.45 kilograms (kg)
2.2 pounds	=	1.0 kilogram

LIQUID VOLUME

1 teaspoon (tsp.)	=	5.0 milliliters (ml)
1 tablespoon (tbsp.)	=	15.0 milliliters
1 fluid ounce (oz.)	=	30.0 milliliters
1 cup (c.)	=	240 milliliters
1 pint (pt.)	=	480 milliliters
1 quart (qt.)	=	0.95 liters (l)
1 gallon (gal.)	=	3.80 liters

LENGTH

¼ inch (in.)	=	0.6 centimeters (cm)
½ inch	=	1.25 centimeters
1 inch	=	2.5 centimeters

TEMPERATURE

212°F	=	100°C (boiling point of water)
225°F	=	110°C
250°F	=	120°C
275°F	=	135°C
300°F	=	150°C
325°F	=	160°C
350°F	=	180°C
375°F	=	190°C
400°F	=	200°C

(To convert temperature in Fahrenheit to Celsius, subtract 32 and multiply by .56)

PAN SIZES

8-inch cake pan	= 20 x 4-centimeter cake pan
9-inch cake pan	= 23 x 3.5-centimeter cake pan
11 x 7-inch baking pan	= 28 x 18-centimeter baking pan
13 x 9-inch baking pan	= 32.5 x 23-centimeter baking pan
9 x 5-inch loaf pan	= 23 x 13-centimeter loaf pan
2-quart casserole	= 2-liter casserole

A Norwegian Table

Norwegians take great pride not only in the preparation of food but also in the table arrangements. Beautiful handwoven table runners are often used instead of full tablecloths. Fresh flowers are on the table in many homes every day during the warmer months of the year. People grow their own flowers or buy them at outdoor flower markets.

Dining out in Norway is expensive, so many people prefer to entertain at home, whether it's an elegant dinner party or a small gathering of friends over a simple meal. It's common to spend a weekend night at a friend's or relative's house, enjoying a long, candlelit dinner with lively conversation.

At the end of a meal, it is polite to tell your host that you have enjoyed the pleasant table setting and the good food. Try serving a Norwegian meal to your family. If you take time and pride in preparing and serving the food, your family will no doubt reward your efforts with a hearty *"Tusen takk!"* ("A thousand thanks!").

A typical Norwegian table is made of wood, and visitors are always welcome at it.

A Norwegian Menu

Most Norwegians eat three meals a day. Breakfast is fairly substantial and often includes cheese, meat or fish, and bread. Lunch is a simple meal, most often open-face sandwiches, while dinner typically includes meat or fish, potatoes, and a vegetable. Below are menu plans for a Norwegian breakfast, lunch, snack, and dinner, along with shopping lists that you'll need to prepare these meals.

BREAKFAST

Rice pudding

Bread (whole wheat or rye)

Slices of cheese (white cheddar or Jarlsberg)

SHOPPING LIST:

Dairy/Egg/Meat

1 qt. milk
light-colored cheese such as white cheddar, Havarti, gouda, or Jarlsberg
1 pt. whipping cream

Canned/Bottled/Boxed

white rice
2 envelopes unflavored gelatin
vanilla extract

Miscellaneous

Bread (whole wheat or rye)
salt
sugar
chopped almonds

*If you plan to do a lot of Norwegian cooking, you may want to stock up on some of the spices commonly used in Scandinavian cooking, such as ground cardamom seed, nutmeg, white pepper, and black peppercorns.

LUNCH

Open-face sandwiches

Fresh fruit

SHOPPING LIST:

Produce

lettuce
1 tomato
1 lemon
1 cucumber
1 bunch of radishes
1 green pepper
fresh dill weed
apples, pears, or other fruit

Dairy/Egg/Meat

butter or margarine
eggs
smoked salmon

white cheddar cheese
Swiss, Havarti, or Jarlsberg
    cheese
sliced ham

Canned/Bottled/Boxed

1 7-oz. can sardines or herring
1 7-oz. can cooked shrimp
Rye crisp crackers
mayonnaise

Miscellaneous

unsliced or thick-sliced bread
paprika

DINNER

Poached salmon

Boiled potatoes

Cucumber salad

Fruit soup

SHOPPING LIST:

Produce

6 medium-sized potatoes, or
    15 to 20 new potatoes
1 bunch of parsley
1 lemon
1 cucumber

Dairy/Egg/Meat

butter or margarine
2 lb. fresh or frozen salmon
    fillets

Canned/Bottled/Boxed

1 1-lb. package pitted prunes
1 9-oz. box raisins
4 oz. dried apricots
1 8¾-oz. can unsweetened
    cherries
tapioca
vinegar

Miscellaneous

salt
black peppercorns*
bay leaf
sugar
white pepper
cinnamon sticks

Lunch / Lunsj

Taking a packed lunch to work or school is a widespread habit in Norway. Everyone from business managers to schoolchildren leaves home with a bag lunch of open-face sandwiches, separated by wax paper. Open-face sandwiches—thick slices of bread spread with butter or mayonnaise and some sort of topping—are very popular throughout Scandinavia. They can be made with many different ingredients.

A leaf of lettuce is placed on bread or rye crisp crackers and topped with a piece of meat, a small fish, a sliced cooked egg or scrambled eggs, liver pâté, or a slice of cheese. Then a small piece of decorative food called a garnish is added. Making open-face sandwiches is an excellent way to use up leftovers. It is also an excellent way to be creative—your sandwiches should not only taste good, but they should look good, too. Try experimenting with different toppings.

A variety of ingredients make open-face sandwiches unique and delicious.
(Recipe on pages 32–33.)

Open-Face Sandwiches/ Smørbrød

Sandwich ingredients:

thickly sliced bread or rye crisp
  crackers*

softened butter or margarine

mayonnaise

lettuce

toppings (meat, cheese, shrimp,
  sardines, smoked salmon)

Garnishes:

*The following ingredients can be
used in various combinations as
garnishes. Use any leftovers in your
next tossed green salad.*

1 tomato

1 lemon, unpeeled

1 cucumber, unpeeled

2 radishes

2 hard-cooked eggs

1 green pepper

paprika

fresh dill weed

To prepare garnishes:

1. Cut tomato into thin wedges about ¼-inch thick at the edge.

2. Wash lemon and cucumber thoroughly and use a sharp knife to slice them as thinly as possible. Make a slit from the edge up to the center of each slice. (The cut edges will be twisted in opposite directions when placed on a sandwich.)

3. Thinly slice radishes and hard-cooked eggs. Clean out and cut green pepper in narrow strips about 2 inches long.

4. Sprinkle a bit of paprika on the yolks of some of the egg slices. Cover garnishes with plastic wrap and refrigerate until you are ready to assemble the sandwiches.

It's common to use different types of bread for smørbrød. The bread must be sturdy and sliced thickly, otherwise it will be too floppy to hold the toppings. For an extra-healthy sandwich, use a whole-grain bread, such as whole wheat or rye, instead of white bread.

Sandwich toppings:

1 7-oz. can of sardines or herring (enough for 7 sandwiches)

1 7-oz. can of tiny cooked shrimp (enough for 5 sandwiches)

boiled ham, thinly sliced (1 slice per sandwich)

smoked salmon (1 slice per sandwich)

2 scrambled eggs (enough for 6 sandwiches)

hard cheese such as Jarlsberg or Swiss (2 slices per sandwich)

1. Gather all your ingredients together.

2. Spread a little butter or mayonnaise thinly on each slice of bread and cover the bread with a lettuce leaf.

3. Add toppings. Arrange the ham or smoked salmon so that there is a fold in the middle. Use a variety of hard cheeses for eye and taste appeal.

4. Put the garnishes on the sandwiches. There is no "right way" to put the filling and garnishes together. The enjoyable part of sandwich making is experimenting with different arrangements. Have fun!

Preparation time: 20 minutes
Makes 1 to 8 sandwiches

Tasty sandwich combinations:

3 sardines, egg slice, green pepper strip, lemon twist

3 herring, egg slice, lemon twist, dill weed

spoonful of shrimp, mayonnaise, cucumber and lemon twisted together, radish slices

boiled ham, egg slice, tomato wedge, cucumber twist

smoked salmon, egg slice, tomato wedge, green pepper strip

cheese, tomato wedge, green pepper strip

scrambled eggs, smoked salmon, dill weed

tomato wedge, cucumber slices, radish slices, green pepper strips

spoonful of shrimp, scrambled eggs, cheese, boiled ham

Potato Soup / *Potetsuppe*

4 medium-sized potatoes

1 onion

½ tsp. salt

2 c. milk

2 tbsp. butter*

½ tbsp. chopped fresh parsley

⅛ tsp. pepper

1. Peel each potato and cut into 4 pieces.

2. Peel onion and chop it well. Put potatoes, onion, and salt in a heavy 2-qt. saucepan. Add enough water to cover the vegetables.

3. Boil until a fork goes into potatoes easily (about 15 to 20 minutes). Do not drain. Mash potatoes and onion in the pan.

4. Add milk slowly, stirring constantly. Allow soup to simmer while you add butter, parsley, and pepper.

5. Stir over medium heat until soup is smooth and hot.

Preparation time: 20 minutes
Cooking time: 40 minutes
Serves 4

*You can leave out the butter in this recipe to cut down on fat.

Eating potato soup is a mouthwatering way to stay warm and full in winter.

Snacks/ *Snack*

For a hearty after-school snack, you may want to try a little *lefse* or some flatbread and cheese with a piece of fruit. Lefse is a soft, pancake-type bread that is usually white with brown "freckles." It may be made with rye or wheat flour, or with potatoes that have been boiled, mashed, and mixed with milk and flour. Lefse can be eaten plain or buttered. When spread with butter and sprinkled with sugar, it's heavenly. Lefse can be found in most grocery stores.

Norwegian flatbread is a thin, crisp, waferlike bread. By itself it is quite bland, but with butter or a piece of cheese it makes a delicious snack. The flatbread recipe in this chapter is quite simple. Flatbread can also be found in most supermarkets.

You may be surprised to find a recipe for waffles in the snack chapter. In Norway waffles are never a breakfast food. Instead, they are eaten as a snack or dessert, served with butter and sugar or with jam or berries and whipped cream or sour cream.

You can also snack on leftover fruit soup or rice pudding (see pages 55 and 69). These treats are just as good on the second or third day as on the first, and it's a nice change to eat them cold.

A quick and easy snack, flatbread is perfect topped with cheese, veggies, or butter. (Recipe on pages 38–39.)

Flatbread / *Flatbrød*

Flatbread is the oldest form of bread in Norway. Traditionally, families baked enough flatbread at one time to last half a year.

1⅓ c. stone-ground whole wheat flour

1⅓ c. all-purpose flour*

¼ c. vegetable oil

1 tsp. baking soda

½ tsp. salt

¾ to 1 c. buttermilk

1. Preheat oven to 350°F. Combine whole wheat flour, all-purpose flour, vegetable oil, baking soda, and salt in a bowl. Mix well.

2. Slowly add just enough buttermilk to make a stiff dough.

3. Knead dough for 30 seconds on a well-floured surface, such as a board or tabletop.

4. Roll a medium-sized handful of dough (about ¼ c.) into a ball and then pat it down into a flat circle. (Cover the remaining dough so it doesn't become too dry.)

5. With a floured rolling pin and on a well-floured surface, roll dough into a very thin 10-inch circle. (If dough is sticking to the surface on which you are working, dust it with more flour.)

6. Place flatbread on an ungreased cookie sheet. To make all your flatbread pieces the same shape and size, score (mark with a deep line) the dough circles with a knife, making triangles, squares, or whatever shapes you prefer. (After baking, the flatbread will be broken into pieces along the scored lines.)

7. Bake at 350°F for 8 to 10 minutes. Flatbread should be crisp and slightly brown around the edges. Cool on a wire rack and repeat with remaining dough.

8. Break flatbread into pieces and serve plain or with desired topping, such as butter or cheese.

Preparation time: 25 minutes
Baking time: 8 to 10 minutes per circle
Makes 9 circles

*For some variations on this recipe, try making flatbread using only white flour or only rye flour. You can also substitute ⅔ c. cornmeal for ⅔ c. flour.

Waffles / Vafler

Norwegian waffle irons make heart-shaped waffles, instead of the square waffles (shown) produced by North American waffle irons.

5 eggs

½ c. sugar

I c. flour

I tsp. ground cardamom seed

¾ c. sour cream

¼ c. butter

1. In a medium mixing bowl, whisk the eggs and sugar for about 5 minutes, or until fluffy.

2. Whisk in the flour, cardamom, and sour cream. Whisk until smooth and creamy.

3. Melt the butter and stir it into the mixture. Set aside for 10 minutes.

4. Spray the waffle iron with nonstick cooking spray, or coat with butter. Cook waffles in the waffle iron according to the manufacturer's instructions. Serve with jam or whipped cream.*

Preparation and cooking time: 25 minutes
Serves 6

*Waffles make a special treat when served with whipped cream and fresh berries. Try blueberries, strawberries, or raspberries.

Dinner/Midday

The evening meal is a special time for families in Norway. Eaten between 6:30 and 7:30 P.M., it is usually the largest meal of the day and often the only hot meal. A home-style Norwegian dinner is hearty and simple. The most important guideline is to use fresh, high-quality ingredients.

Dinners usually include meat or fish as a main course, along with boiled potatoes or another vegetable and perhaps a salad. Lamb, mutton, and pork are the most popular meats, although Norwegians also eat beef, chicken, and even reindeer meat. Common meat dishes include meatcakes, which are sort of like meatballs; pork sausage patties; and lamb and cabbage stew. Dinner could also be a substantial soup or an egg dish.

Like other Norwegian foods, desserts are influenced by the seasons. In the summer, many Norwegians eat fresh berries every day. Dessert might be plain fruit, fruit soup, or apple cake. Fancier desserts, such as whipped cream cake, are served at parties and celebrations.

Fish and produce available at Norwegian markets make poached salmon and boiled potatoes a fresh and flavorful dinner. (Recipes on pages 44 and 45.)

Poached Salmon / *Kokt Laks*

Poaching is one of the easiest and most popular ways to cook fish. Poaching simply means to cook in a simmering liquid, usually water with salt and sometimes vinegar, wine, or broth. Salmon, trout, cod, and halibut are good poached and can be cooked whole or in pieces. Poached fish may be served warm or cold and is often accompanied by a sauce or melted butter. Boiled potatoes and cucumber salad are traditional accompaniments to poached fish.

About 2 lb. salmon fillets (thaw if frozen)

Cooking liquid:

1 qt. water

2 tbsp. salt

1 tbsp. vinegar

juice of one lemon

3 to 4 whole peppercorns

1 stalk of parsley

1 bay leaf

1. Wash the fish under cold water and pat dry with paper towels. Cut into 1-inch-thick slices. In a stockpot or large saucepan, combine water, salt, vinegar, lemon juice, peppercorns, parsley, and bay leaf. Bring to a boil. Reduce heat and simmer liquid about 10 minutes.

2. Place the fish slices into the simmering water and cook about 8 to 10 minutes, until the flesh flakes easily. Remove fish from pot with a slotted spoon.

3. Serve fish warm with lemon wedges, melted butter, boiled potatoes, and cucumber salad (recipe on page 51), or chill and serve cold with a green salad.

Preparation time: 15 minutes
Cooking time: 25 minutes
Serves 4

Boiled Potatoes / *Kokte Poteter*

Parsley is a favorite garnish for boiled potatoes. In the summer, Norwegians grow their own parsley outside, and in the winter they grow it in small indoor pots placed near a window.

6 medium-sized potatoes*

I tsp. salt

2 tbsp. butter or margarine

I tbsp. chopped fresh parsley

1. Peel potatoes and place them in a pan of cold, salted water. (The water should just cover potatoes.)

2. Cover the pan and place over high heat. Allow potatoes to boil until tender (about 15 to 20 minutes). When a fork goes into potatoes easily, drain off water.

3. Put the lid back on the pan and return to the stove to keep warm. (Make sure that the burner under the pan is off.) Add butter or margarine and parsley before serving.

Preparation time: 15 minutes
Cooking time: 20 minutes
Serves 6

*Instead of using medium-sized potatoes, try using new potatoes—young, small potatoes with thin skins. Leave the skin on the new potatoes when you cook and eat them—it adds to the flavor and texture.

Baked Cod/ *Ovnstekt Torsk*

Fish is served often in Norway, and it is prepared in many ways. It can be baked, poached in water, fried, combined with potatoes, onions, and flour into fishballs, or cooked in a casserole with white sauce and bread crumbs.

6 cod fillets (thaw if frozen)

4 c. hot milk (enough to barely cover the fish)

6 tsp. butter or margarine

1. Preheat the oven to 350°F.

2. Grease a shallow baking dish or a 9 × 13-inch pan. Arrange fillets, placing them close together in the dish or pan. (Choose a baking container in which fillets will fit closely together.)

3. Pour enough hot milk over fish to barely cover fillets.

4. Top each fillet with a teaspoon of butter or margarine. Bake for 20 minutes, or until fish flakes easily when tested with a fork.

Preparation time: 10 minutes
Baking time: 20 minutes
Serves 4 to 6

Sprinkling baked cod with fresh parsley gives it more texture and color.

Meatcakes / Kjøttkaker

Most Norwegians rank meatcakes as one of the country's most typical dishes.

1 lb. lean or extra-lean ground beef

1½ tsp. salt

¼ tsp. pepper

¼ tsp. nutmeg

¼ tsp. ginger

2½ tbsp. potato flour or cornstarch

about ¾ c. skim milk or water

1 tbsp. butter or oil for frying*

1 to 2 c. water, beef bouillon, or milk

Gravy:

1 to 2 tbsp. flour

salt and pepper to taste

2 tbsp. onion, finely chopped

1. In a mixing bowl, work the salt into the meat until the mixture becomes sticky. Next, work in the pepper, nutmeg, ginger, and potato flour or cornstarch. Gradually add the milk or water.

2. Shape the meat into round patties. Fry them in a little butter or oil in a hot frying pan.

3. When patties are browned, transfer them to a pan with 1 to 2 c. of boiling water, beef bouillon, or milk. Lower heat and simmer patties until done, about 10 to 15 minutes. Remove from pan with slotted spoon.

4. To make a gravy for the meatcakes, blend a tablespoon or two of flour with a little cold water and add it to the water or bouillon used to cook the meatcakes. Stir until thickened, adding more flour if necessary, and season to taste with salt, pepper, and finely chopped onion.

5. Serve the meatcakes with boiled potatoes and peas.

*To reduce the saturated fat in this recipe, fry the meatcakes in a vegetable oil, such as corn, safflower, or canola, rather than in butter.

Preparation time: 15 minutes
Cooking time: 20 minutes
Serves 4

Mashed Rutabagas / *Kålrotstappe*

Many people avoid rutabagas, either because they've never had them or they think they don't taste good. But this simple rutabaga dish has a tasty, mild flavor. And rutabagas supply a healthy dose of vitamins, minerals, and calcium. The rutabaga's popularity in Scandinavia earned it the nickname "swede" or the "orange of the North."

1½ lb. rutabagas

1 large potato

1 tsp. salt

salt and pepper to taste

3 to 4 tbsp. milk

1. Peel the rutabagas and potato. Slice rutabagas and place them with the whole potato in a pan of cold, salted water (just enough water to cover the vegetables). Bring water to a boil and cook vegetables until tender. Carefully pour off the water and let any remaining moisture steam off.

2. Mash potato and rutabagas together, season to taste with salt and pepper, and add milk until the mixture has the desired consistency. Reheat and serve piping hot.

Preparation time: 15 minutes
Cooking time: 20 to 30 minutes
Serves 4

Cucumber Salad / Agurksalat

Cucumber salad is eaten in all Scandinavian countries. The cucumbers must be sliced paper thin! A Norwegian cheese slicer works well for this.

1 cucumber*

2 tsp. vinegar

½ tsp. salt

1 tsp. sugar

¼ tsp. white pepper

chopped parsley, chives, or dill weed

1. Slice the cucumber paper thin.

2. Mix vinegar, salt, sugar, and pepper in a small bowl and pour over cucumber slices.

3. Sprinkle with parsley, chives, or dill weed before serving.

Preparation time: 10 minutes
Serves 4 to 6

This salad is best made with European or Asian cucumbers. These are longer and thinner than the ordinary variety sold in the United States, and they have few or no seeds. Usually sold in a plastic covering, they are more expensive than regular cucumbers, but the taste is worth it.

Beet Patties / *Rødbetekarbonader*

These patties are a vegetarian alternative to meatcakes. Make some of each to please both your meat-eating and vegetarian friends!

3 to 4 large beets

1½ tsp. salt

3 large potatoes

2 stalks of celery, chopped

2 eggs

2 tbsp. dried bread crumbs*

¼ tsp. pepper

1 tbsp. butter or oil for frying

1. Place beets in a pan of cold, salted water. (The water should just cover beets.) Bring to a boil and cook until tender (a fork should go into the beets easily). Next, boil potatoes until tender, and boil celery until tender. (You can use three pots and cook all vegetables separately at the same time, or use one pot and boil them separately in turn.) When all the vegetables are cooked, peel and mash the beets and potatoes and mix them together with the celery.

2. In a large mixing bowl, beat eggs and mix them with bread crumbs. Let mixture stand and swell a little before adding the vegetables. Mix all together well. Season with salt and pepper.

3. Heat butter or oil in a frying pan. Use a large spoon or your hand to form the vegetable mixture into flat patties and place them in the pan. Brown patties on both sides.

*You can buy bread crumbs prepackaged at the supermarket, or you can make your own. To make your own, whirl slices of any bread you have on hand in a blender or food processor for several seconds. You can also crumble the bread into crumbs by hand.

Preparation time: 1 hour
Cooking time: 20 minutes
Serves 4

Fruit Soup/Fruktsuppe

This dessert soup is spicy and refreshing. Try serving it cold with a dollop of low-fat or nonfat plain yogurt on top.

1 1-lb. package pitted prunes

1½ c. raisins

1 cinnamon stick

6 c. water

4 oz. (1 c.) dried apricots

1 8¾-oz. can unsweetened cherries and juice

3 tbsp. quick-cooking tapioca

¼ c. sugar

1. Put prunes, raisins, cinnamon sticks, and water in a large, heavy kettle. Bring to a boil, then reduce heat and simmer about 30 minutes, or until prunes and raisins are soft.

2. Add apricots and cook for 10 minutes, or until they are plump and soft.

3. Pour off liquid from cooked fruit into another kettle. (You may need help from a friend when you do this.) Add juice from cherries to liquid. Then add tapioca and sugar. Cook over medium heat, stirring often, until tapioca is clear. The juice should be thick by this time. (You will have to cook the mixture for at least 30 minutes to get clear tapioca and thickened juice.)

4. Remove cinnamon stick from fruit. Add thickened juice and cherries to fruit. Stir. You can add slices of oranges and lemons to this mixture for color. Serve warm or cold.

Preparation and cooking time: 1½ hours
Serves 12

Slices of oranges or lemons give this distinctive dessert more color.

Whipped Cream Cake/Bløtkake

This layer cake is the most popular cake in Norway. It is often part of a holiday or family celebration or is served to company. It makes a delicious and attractive birthday cake.

Cake:

4 large eggs, at room temperature

1 c. sugar

1 tsp. vanilla extract

1 c. flour

1 tsp. baking powder

Filling:

1 to 2 c. heavy (whipping) cream

2 tbsp. powdered sugar

1 tsp. vanilla extract

about ¼ c. fruit juice (use the type of fruit that's in the cake)

1 qt. fresh strawberries or other fruit, sliced

1. Preheat oven to 350°F. Spray two 9-inch round cake pans with nonstick cooking spray. Using an electric mixer, beat the eggs until frothy. Add sugar gradually, beating until very thick and lemon colored, scraping the sides of the bowl often. Blend in vanilla extract.

2. In a separate bowl, stir together the flour and baking powder. Fold dry ingredients into the egg mixture. Mix until just blended.

3. Pour batter into the two prepared cake pans, spreading it to the edges. Bake for 25 to 30 minutes, or until the center of the cake bounces back when touched. Remove the cake layers from the oven and cool.

4. To prepare the filling, whip the cream with an electric mixer until stiff peaks form. Add sugar and vanilla extract.

5. Remove the cooled cakes from the pans. Turn one layer onto a serving plate so that the flat side is face up (the brown, top side will be down).

6. Sprinkle a little fruit juice over the bottom layer of the cake.* Spread the layer with half of the whipped cream and cover with a generous layer of strawberries (or other fruit).

7. Place the second layer of cake over the strawberries so that the flat side is face up. Sprinkle this layer with a little fruit juice, then spread the remaining whipped cream and strawberries on it. Serve immediately, or refrigerate up to 2 hours, then serve.

Preparation time: 30 minutes
Baking time: 25 to 30 minutes
Assembly time: 10 minutes
Serves 8 to 12

*The basic layers of cake are easy to make and can be filled with anything you like, including jam and any type of berry or other fruit, in addition to the whipped cream.

Holiday and Festival Food

Everyone in Norway looks forward to holidays and festivals as a time to see family and friends, spend time outdoors, and enjoy an abundance of good food. Baking and preparing special foods is a major part of some holidays, such as Christmas, and many recipes have been passed down for generations. Other holidays, such as Easter, have no particular foods associated with them. Holiday foods vary from one region to another.

Perhaps the most traditional holiday food is rømmegrøt. This rich "velvet porridge" is served on many holidays, especially Midsummer Eve and Olsok (Saint Olav's Day). It is usually eaten with cinnamon and sugar.

The following recipes have special connections to particular holidays, but Norwegians eat these foods at other times of the year, too. If you like one of these recipes, you can add it to your year-round menu!

Rice pudding topped with raspberry sauce is a sure sign of Christmas in Norway. (Recipes on pages 68 and 69.)

Smoked Salmon Quiche/ *Røkelaksterte*

Pastry ingredients:

1¾ c. flour

8 oz. (1 stick) unsalted butter

up to ½ c. water

Filling ingredients:

½ c. finely chopped onion

2½ tbsp. butter or margarine, cut into pieces

14 oz. chopped smoked salmon

2 tsp. chopped fresh chives

½ clove garlic, chopped

2 tsp. chopped fresh basil

5 eggs

2 c. milk

pepper to taste

1. Quickly combine flour, butter, and water in a food processor. Gather pastry dough into a ball, cover with plastic wrap, and chill 1 hour. (If you do not have a food processor, use your hands or a fork to mix the flour and butter together until mixture is crumbly. Add water a little at a time, using just enough to allow the dough to form a ball.)

2. Preheat the oven to 400°F. Roll out dough and place in a 10-inch pie pan. Prick with a fork a few times. Bake 10 minutes. Remove from oven and reduce oven temperature to 325°F.

3. Sauté onion in the butter or margarine until translucent. Stir in salmon, chives, garlic, and basil. Remove from heat and cool.

4. Arrange the salmon mixture in the pastry shell. Whisk eggs with milk, season with pepper to taste, and pour over salmon mixture.

5. Bake about 30 minutes, or until quiche is puffed and golden. Allow to cool for 10 to 15 minutes before serving.

Preparation time: 2 hours
(including 1 hour for pastry to chill)
Baking time: 30 minutes
Serves 8

Sour Cream Porridge / *Rømmegrøt*

Sour cream porridge is one of the oldest recipes in Norway. It's always been served on special occasions, including birthdays, weddings, and baptisms. It was traditionally given as a gift to a hostess or a new mother. Many people eat rømmegrøt with dried or cured meats. Although Norwegians consider rømmegrøt a main dish, it makes a wonderful dessert when served with a sprinkling of cinnamon and sugar.

2 c. sour cream

¾ c. flour

2 c. milk

dash of salt

cinnamon and sugar, for serving

1. In a heavy-bottomed saucepan, bring sour cream to a boil. Boil for 2 minutes, stirring frequently, then add half the flour and stir or whisk it carefully. Skim off the butter (from the sour cream) that rises to the surface, put it in a pan or bowl, and keep it warm.

2. Stir in the rest of the flour, one tablespoon at a time. Stir in the milk. Simmer, whisking, for 5 to 6 minutes, until the porridge is very smooth. Season to taste with salt.

3. Serve with the reserved warm butter and cinnamon and sugar. A red fruit juice, such as raspberry, is usually drunk with the porridge.

Preparation and cooking time: 20 minutes
Serves 6 to 8

Centuries of tradition have made sour cream porridge a beloved Norwegian dish.

Christmas Bread/Julekake

Christmas bread is delicious with breakfast, and it makes wonderful toast.

1 c. raisins

1 c. candied red and green cherries or assorted candied fruit, cut in small pieces

2 tbsp. active dry yeast

1 tbsp. sugar

¼ c. warm water

2 c. milk

½ c. shortening

½ c. sugar

2 tsp. salt

2 tsp. ground cardamom seed

6½ c. all-purpose flour

½ c. blanched almonds, finely chopped

additional all-purpose flour (½ to 1½ c.)

1. Soften raisins by putting them in a small amount of hot water. Prepare cherries or candied fruit by shaking them in a bag with a little flour. Set raisins and cherries aside.

2. In a glass measuring cup or drinking glass, dissolve yeast and 1 tbsp. sugar in ¼ c. warm water.

3. In a saucepan, scald milk. Stir in shortening and let cool for 15 minutes. When cooled, pour milk and shortening in a big mixing bowl. Add sugar, salt, and cardamom and stir.

4. With a mixing spoon, stir in 2 c. of the flour, 1 c. at a time. Next, add yeast, sugar, and water mixture. Stir, then add 2 more cups flour, stirring. Add candied fruit, raisins, and chopped almonds, mixing well. Stir in 2 c. of remaining flour, 1 c. at a time.

5. Turn dough onto a floured board and knead well. Use as much remaining flour as it takes to reach a springy, elastic texture. Place dough in a greased bowl and cover with a damp cloth.

6. Put dough in a warm place (about 80°F) or in a closed oven (turned off) with a pan of hot water beneath on the bottom rack. Let dough rise until doubled in size. Punch down and let rise until doubled again. (Each rising should take about 45 minutes.)

7. Punch down dough and cut into two equal sections.

8. Knead each section well. Form two round loaves and place them on a cookie sheet. Cover with a damp cloth and let rise for about 30 minutes.

9. Preheat the oven to 350°F. (Be sure to remove the two loaves first if you have put them in the oven to rise!)

10. Bake loaves for about 35 minutes, or until tops are golden brown.*

Preparation time: 1 hour
Rising time: 2 hours
Baking time: 35 minutes
Makes 2 round loaves

*You can eat this bread warm or cold. Try it with a slice of mild cheese or with butter and jam.

Gingerbread Cookies / *Pepperkaker*

These gingerbread men and women can be hung on the Christmas tree, if you can resist eating them.

1 c. butter

2 c. sugar

½ c. molasses

2 eggs

3 tbsp. vinegar

4½ c. flour

3 tsp. baking soda

1 tsp. baking powder

½ tsp. white pepper

1 tsp. ginger

1 tsp. cinnamon

1. Preheat oven to 375°F.

2. In a large mixing bowl, cream together butter and sugar until light and fluffy.

3. Add molasses, eggs, and vinegar and mix well.

4. In a separate bowl, blend flour, baking soda, baking powder, white pepper, ginger, and cinnamon.

5. Add flour mixture to the butter and sugar, stirring until well mixed.

6. Turn dough onto a well-floured board. Using a floured rolling pin, roll out dough thinly. Cut into desired shapes with cookie cutters.* (If you don't have cookie cutters, you can use a glass to make circles.) Using a spatula, transfer cookies to ungreased cookie sheets.

7. Bake for 9 to 11 minutes, until puffy and lightly browned. (Repeat with remaining cookies.)

*You can decorate your gingerbread people with frosting. Put 3 tbsp. hot water in a small bowl. Beat in 2½ c. confectioner's (powdered) sugar until the frosting is thick enough to spread. Continue to beat for several minutes until very creamy. Spread on cookies.

Preparation time: 20 minutes
Baking time: 9 to 11 minutes
Makes 50 to 75 cookies

Raspberry Sauce / *Rødsaus*

1 10-oz. package frozen raspberries (with syrup), thawed

½ c. apple or currant jelly

1 tbsp. cold water

1½ tsp. cornstarch

1. In a saucepan, bring raspberries (with syrup) and jelly to a boil. Turn off heat.

2. Combine water and cornstarch in a bowl. Then stir mixture into raspberries.

3. Return to a boil, stirring constantly.

4. Boil and stir for 1 minute.

5. Serve warm sauce on top of cold rice pudding.

Preparation and cooking time: 10 minutes
Serves 8

Rice Pudding / *Riskrem*

Gelatin is an animal product, made from animal bones and tissue. A vegetarian alternative to regular gelatin is agar-agar, a gelatin made from sea vegetables. It is sold in bar form, as a powder, or in flakes.

½ c. water

2 envelopes unflavored gelatin

½ c. sugar

½ tsp. salt

2 c. milk*

1½ c. cooked white rice

2 tsp. vanilla extract

¼ c. chopped almonds

1 c. chilled whipping cream, or nonfat dairy topping

1. In a saucepan, heat water, gelatin, sugar, and salt. Stir constantly until gelatin is dissolved (about 1 minute).

2. Stir in milk, rice, vanilla extract, and almonds.

3. Place the saucepan in a bowl of ice water, stirring occasionally for about 15 minutes. (Mixture should form a slight lump when dropped from a spoon.)

4. Beat whipping cream until stiff and fold into rice mixture.

5. Pour into an ungreased 1½-qt. mold. Cover and chill until set (about 3 hours).

6. Turn out and serve cold with raspberry sauce.

Preparation time: 25 minutes (plus 3 hours to chill)
Serves 8

*The pudding will taste just as good, but less rich, if you use skim milk in place of whole milk.

Index

About the Author

Sylvia Munsen, a third-generation Norwegian American, was raised in Story City, Iowa, a community of Norwegian descendants. She grew up eating many traditional Norwegian foods and singing Norwegian folk songs with her grandmother.

Munsen graduated from St. Olaf College in Northfield, Minnesota, where she earned a degree in music education and was a member of the St. Olaf choir. She also studied Norwegian language and literature at the University of Oslo International Summer School.

Photo Acknowledgments
The photographs in this book are reproduced courtesy of: © Wolfgang Kaehler, pp. 2–3, 11, 15, 26; © Walter and Louiseann Pietrowicz/September 8th Stock, pp. 4 (left and right), 5 (left and right), 6, 18, 30, 35, 36, 41, 42, 47, 48, 53, 54, 58, 61, 62, 67; Adam Woolfitt/CORBIS, p. 12; Dave G. Houser/CORBIS, p. 16.

Cover photos: © Walter and Louiseann Pietrowicz/September 8th Stock (front top and back); © Robert L. and Diane Wolfe (front bottom and spine).

The illustrations on pp. 7, 19, 27, 28, 31, 32, 34, 37, 39, 40, 43, 45, 49, 51, 52, 57, 59, 65, 66, 69 and the map on page 8 are by Tim Seeley.